Shadows & Mirror

Liora Johnson

Presentation by *BookLeaf Publishing*

Web: www.bookleafpub.com

E-mail: info@bookleafpub.com

ISBN: 978-93-95890-77-9

First edition 2022

DEDICATION

This book is dedicated to Shawn & Tanya Johnson, Isabel Dekrey, Andy & Ashley Mason, Tim & Tina Stilwell, Sandy & Russ Johnson, Valerie & Lou Rondeau, and all of the other wonderful people who have been waiting for me to publish something.

ACKNOWLEDGEMENT

I draw inspiration from the greats (J. R. R. Tolkien, Lewis Carol, and C. S. Lewis), while fully embracing my own unique style and literary voice, which is quite different from theirs.

PREFACE

Life can be humorous, and life can be dark.
I strive to write the best of both worlds.

In Search of a Rainbow

Pastel clouds on a crimson tide,
Ebbing and weaving, though sometimes they
hide
Behind the trees and sun on high,
Chasing and seeking the glimmers of light.

Soaring and dipping through the mist,
Across the wilds with a silver-clad fist,
They hunt for an item of bliss;
A rainbow of pure lofty looks and light.

The Little Snake's Journey

Shadows veiled the marshes,
The murky water bubbled and foamed.
A long, slimy snake was finding its way
To the grasslands where pig-turtles moaned.

The snake had found its way up past
The rocky cliffs and crashing waves.
It dared not look down for fear, because
He would certainly meet with his grave.

The snake carried on relentlessly,
He just had to get to his goal!
But t'was late at night, and the snake was tired;
His blood was getting real cold.

So the snake curled up in a tree,
Hoping nobody would find him.
The grasslands were still so far away,
And the chances he'd get there were grim.

The snake kept on slithering well into noon,
Though the lands here were withered and bleak,
But he mumbled a prayer (as best a snake
could),
As he slithered, his wishes so meek.

The snake carried on, straight through oceans,
Where fish-cats and sea-giraffes played.
He carried on through the old forest,
And he carried on through the white glades.

Finally, then, he could see it;
The grasslands with beautiful lakes.
Alas, poor thing, he would loved to have stayed,
But a pig-turtle stepped on the snake.

Mortality

Ebbing and flowing,
Life is a bloom;
A flower that shrivels and rots.

Rising and falling,
Life is a sea;
A tide that is there, then is not.

The Flood

Panic seized the people,
Thunder growled in the sky,
Flashes of lighting cut the night
And hope of escape had flown by.

Rain whizzed through the air to the ground,
A flood commenced to grow.
The earth called out a shuddering moan
As the downpour continued to flow.

The lake in the streets was knee-high now,
But the raining didn't stop;
A few fated houses bore metal roofs,
And lightning crashed on their tops.

Crows were calling loudly
As the water grew steadily higher.
Then a snap, a crack, a loud, painful scream,
And a few low grumbles of thunder.

The rain had stopped, homes now wrecked,
Debris had scattered the streets.
Only the roofers were happy, because,
T'was certain the roofs would have leaks.

No one could handle this trauma;
Too much had been lost to the flood.
Each house and shed was utterly rent,
And was totally coated in mud.

We'll never forget that horrible day
That we lost our homes to the rain.
I can still hear the screams, I can still see the fear,
And I certainly still feel the pain.

The Villain's Heart

Her eyes, a plaintive hue,
Etched their ways into my mind,
Gaining upon me a strangle-hold,
And giving me feelings sublime.

The soft voice, sounding so kind,
Her darling words eating my soul,
My fingers went numb and my spirit erect
As I stroked her hair, black as coal.

If only she knew what a monster I've been,
How I'd foolishly given my life
To emptier words, to menacing thoughts,
And was now barricaded with strife.

Is there a way to spare her the tears?
Alas, what a grievous thought!
The things that I've done, the sorrow I bring,
And a happier life I've not sought.

She truly adores me, that much I can tell,
But her number-one fan I am not;
She stands here, blinded to all of my flaws,
Unaware of my devious thoughts.

To save her from woe- an impossible task-
To spare her the pain, I cannot.
She will have to face it; I am not a kind man,
And an era of pain I have wrought.

I flee, then, although
My heart pleads to stay.
To stay would be foolish;
A price I can't pay.

Devastation

Rain and snow,
Ice cascades
Down a steep mountain crest
And into the glade.

Peace and joy,
All are lost
As they run from the glade,
Not thinking of cost.

Thunder strikes,
Dark times fall
On the village of men,
With anger toward all.

Starlight fades,
Skies, now black,
Hang ominous o'er them
And bright lightning cracks.

Hope is lost
As night falls,
And possessions, destroyed,
Lie in crumbled walls.

Silence falls.

A Tear

Shattered sunsets fade into rivers,
Veiling the truth underlying,
Night, a blanket of impending doom, is released
And forfeits all hope of being revealed.

Lo, the ivory basing that collects the rain,
A solemn face, a mortal gesture,
Is in overflow with the trickling poison,
Toxic to the touch and taste.

Here you can almost feel the agony,
The tremendous turmoil of woe,
The beating heart, rasping breath,
Stricken to the bone with immortal sorrow.

Fire like ice, it claws at the mind,
Itching to spring forth and attack.
Begging "Release!" as it dies in its cell,
Until its burning grows too much to bear.

It forces its way, slicing out of the brain,
It gnashes its fangs in despair.
It's ready, it's here; it's finally free,
And now, you are shedding the tear.

Nightfall

A charred horizon slithered onto the palette of
dawn,
Veiling the vision of light and warmth.
Sunshine is banished and darker dreams slip
through the heavens.

Fractured whisperings spew from the mourning
lark,
Whose eyes yearn for the glassy parchment to
fall and swallow him.
Yea, even the seas shriek in agony at the thought
of the sun's exile.

The shadows of night pour into the moorlands,
Hunting their prey under the blanket of
darkness.
The phantoms prowl, not ceasing to drag out
terror from our souls.

Coal-dust skirts plummet now into a dreary
abyss,
The white bird tempestuously cries her sister's
loss.

Black scales fall into our eyes, and the shining
light is no more.

The Viper's Dinner

Coiled in darkness, it watches
Waiting for prey to pass by.
Seeing the victim, it lunges;
Blood is then spilled in the night.

Against a shadowed backdrop,
It sits in silence- alone-
While its meal congeals in its stomach;
After this, it spits out the bones.

When the meal is all finished, it studies
The clouds and the grass and the sky.
What a beautiful place for its dinner;
But alas, it is colorblind.

Battle for the Warrior's Land

They call to the shadow, seeking refuge in its
calm,
Yearning to find resolve in the blissful gloom.
Hearken your ears, warriors of old;
To take back your land, your hearts must be
bold.

They march into warfare, finding death scattered
abroad,
Desperate to discover some form of life in the
chaos.
Hearken your ears, warriors of old;
To take back your land, your hearts must be
bold.

Lo, a single butterfly scans the field that's
battle-torn,
Longing for its family to be reunited unto it.
Hearken your ears, warriors of old;
To take back your land, your hearts must be
bold.

They cry from the gullies, the caverns, the
graves,

They cry their battle song as they strive for victory.
Hearken your ears, warriors of old;
To take back your land, your hearts must be bold.

Finally silence, a beautiful utterance to the soldier's ears.
The battle was over! Victory rung bold in the heavens.
Sound the trumpets, warriors of old;
Your swords proved strong, and your hearts are bold.

My Savior

Rumbling thunder crashed down from the sky,
Stormy horizons are brewing on high.
Visions of shadow and lightning and woe
Seep into my soul; yea, my heart has sunk low.

Merciless echos awaiting my fall,
Waiting for me- all my failures to call.
Tasting my fear, they surround me again;
Looking upon me with grim, twisted grins.

Now I can feel them all around me,
Chortling madly with unconstrained glee.
Now I have fallen, broken and bruised;
All of my fears now upon me are loosed.

Then I look up at the dark, gloomy sky,
A woeful gray tear sliding down from my eye.
I beg for a savior; I silently call...
And then I could see Him- angels and all!

He killed off my shadows, He chased off my
fears,
He knelt down beside me and wiped off my
tears.
The prince of my demons, now mad in his rage,

Had come down to take me away to my grave.

My Savior stood up, a sword in His hand,
And held up a shield made of silver so grand.
He struck down the prince of the shadow and
gloom,
He saved me from death and my impending
doom.

He secured me a future in true paradise,
And now I am free; yes, I'm free from all strife!
Now I will serve Him the rest of my days,
Serving Jesus, my Savior; my soul He did save!

The Trapped Memory

Shattering, shaking,
Shivering, breaking,
Clawing its way out of darkness.

Shimmering cave light,
Searching for daylight,
Looking for one thing: the surface.

Quivering moonlight,
Secret to all sight,
Wandering through the shadows.

Echoing Madly,
Hair, gnarled and ratty,
Running through endless mineshafts.

Gravely it ponders,
Looking far yonder,
Longing to find its freedom.

Gruesome, it cries,
Forlorn, it sighs,
Searching about for exit.

Wanting for rescue,

Broken it tells you,
There may be no hope for escape.

Begging for someone,
Day passing far on,
Seething, it clashes its fangs.

Writhing with fury,
Wishing it to be
Free from this endless prison.

Here it is silent,
Recalling vibrant
When it was free from its place.

The Soldier's Death

The war raged on around me,
I saw the wounded die,
I heard the screams, I saw the fear,
And all I could do was cry.

The clouds poured rain to wash away
The blood that poured from men,
The sky was black with misery;
Black as a lion's den.

A sword swept through the valley,
Another twenty died.
A seething pain, a shuddering child-
All hope I had was fried.

A blow to the head sends me reeling back,
An arrow embeds in my chest.
I feel the life being sucked from me
As I lay in painful rest.

My sword is taken from its sheath;
It's used to slay my friends.
I let a tear drip down my face
As my life eventually ends.

The Young Bard

Singing a sonnet, nay, ballad of truth,
Came a sprightly young wandering bard-like
youth.
He held in his hands both a fiddle and harp,
With which he could play and sing songs like a
lark.

He traveled abroad and his name became great,
So the wealthy old king calls upon him of late
To hear his magnificent singing of songs,
As the music is soothing and brings peace in
throngs.

The traveling bard never asked for money,
Though his playing was sweet and his voice was
like honey.
This only made people adore him the more,
And they'd gather to listen to him on the shore.

On the shore of the ocean he'd play and he'd
sing,
With melodious voice, pure as a gold ring.
He'd laugh and he'd jest with his mirthful
crowd,
That had gathered around

Just to hear his sound.

The Aftermath of a Dragon

Blackened walls and broken homes
Herald the dragon's might.
It ravaged the whole of our little old town
In the middle of the night.

We tried to run, we tried to hide,
But the dragon came and killed.
It slaughtered our families, animals, lives,
And into our hearts sorrow drilled.

Will You Follow the King?

Have you ever danced with the angels?
Have you praised your Creator aloud?
Have you come before Him, a smile on your
face,
And lifted your hands to the clouds?

Have you worshiped The LORD in your
actions?
Have you lived your life unto Him?
Have you tried to follow His guidance and will
And followed the path ever slim?

Your life, a fleeting vapor,
Could be used to bring glory to God...
Or you could go down the sinister path
Which so many people would trod.

That path will bring no fulfillment;
It's a dark and painful life.
But turn now to God and let Him take over,
And He will get rid of your strife.

"Follow Me Now!"

She heard the voice calling her name;
It promised her riches and fame.
It cried out in such a loud voice,
"Follow me, follow me now!"

The offer, too good to be true,
Left a doubt in her through and through.
It sobbed and it swore at her then,
"Follow me, follow me now!"

She did not want to follow it,
For she felt it was all a trick.
The voice, now burning with anger,
Screamed "Follow me! Follow me now!"

Shielding her ears from the loud voice,
She fled from there by her own choice.
She could hear it chasing her down,
With the screech of "Follow me now!"

"Follow me!"

"Follow me!"

"Follow me now!"

The voice was fading away.
As she fled from the whispers
Inside of the dark,
She emerged into glorious day.

The Death of Imagination

Her friends were all but dead;
Once visible creatures that surrounded her were
gone,
And she was left in silence and misery.

There was naught but a dark hole in her heart
Where her companions once dwelled;
Now that they were gone, she began to cry.

The people around her scoffed as they saw her
tears,
But she did not pay heed to them-
She felt no embarrassment; only pain.

"They were not real," said the people,
But they were very real to her.
She felt no anger; only anguish.

With imagination as dead as her friends,
She rose to her feet and sighed;
She would have to give them up to be accepted.

9 789395 890779